HAULING PROFITS

Launching Your Prosperous Truck Business from Ground Up, Securing Clients, and Navigating Logistics for Long-Term Success

OSCAR MOSES

Hauling Profits
© Copyright 2024 by Oscar Moses
All rights reserved

The information provided herein is stated to be truthful and consistent, in that any liability, in terms of inattention or otherwise, by any usage or abuse of any policies, processes, or directions contained within is the solitary and utter responsibility of the recipient reader. Under no circumstances will any legal responsibility or blame be held against the publisher for any reparation, damages, or monetary loss due to the information herein, either directly or indirectly.

Respective authors own all copyrights not held by the publisher.

The information herein is offered for informational purposes solely, and is universal as so. The presentation of the information is without contract or any type of guarantee assurance.

The trademarks that are used are without any consent, and the publication of the trademark is without permission or backing by the trademark owner. All trademarks and brands within this book are for clarifying purposes only and are owned by the owners themselves, not affiliated with this document.

TABLE OF CONTENTS

INTRODUCTION

Welcome to the World of Trucking Business

So you want to get into the trucking industry? Congratulations on setting your sights on this exciting and ever-growing business. As a beginner, the world of trucking can seem daunting. But with the right knowledge, planning, and passion, you can pave the road to success. In this chapter, we'll explore the basics of starting your own trucking company and share tips to help you navigate the first miles of your journey.

Selecting Your Specialty

Before purchasing your first rig, determine what type of freight you want to haul. Some common trucking niches include:

- Dry van - General consumer goods and materials. A versatile option to start.

- Refrigerated - Perishable foods and frozen items. Requires a refrigerated trailer.

- Tanker - Liquids like fuel, milk, or chemicals. Need specialty tank trailers.

- Flatbed - Construction equipment or oddly shaped loads. Open-air flatbed trailers.

Research your local market to see what shippers and routes are in highest demand. Specializing makes it easier to market your services. And less competition means higher profits.

Buying Your Truck

As an owner-operator, your truck is your most critical business asset. So choose it wisely:

- Buy used at first. Opt for a model no older than 5 years to balance cost savings with safety.

- Look for fuel efficiency. Newer trucks boast better gas mileage. Save money at the pump.

- Do a comprehensive inspection. Check the engine, tires, and components before purchasing.

- Obtain financing if needed. Many dealers offer payment plans or leasing options.

A well-maintained truck will provide many reliable miles out on the open highway. Perform regular maintenance and promptly address any issues that arise.

Developing a Business Plan

Like any venture, a trucking company requires careful planning and number crunching:

- Research all costs - Factoring in expenses for fuel, insurance, maintenance, and more will give you an accurate financial picture. Don't leave anything out!

- Set competitive rates - Underbid and you lose profits. Overbid and you lose jobs. Price your services fairly based on industry standards.

- Fundraise working capital - Starting a business takes a sizable upfront investment. Seek loans or investors to cover these early costs.

- Obtain licenses - Register your business, apply for operating authority, and comply with all federal and state regulations.

Having a well-developed business plan establishes a course towards profitability and prevents your company from veering off track.

Building Customer Relationships

One of the most important aspects of the trucking business is building strong customer relationships:

- Network at local shippers - Introduce yourself in person as a reliable new provider in town.

- Join industry groups - Being active in trade associations boosts visibility and connections.

- Provide exceptional service - Exceed expectations by delivering shipments on-time with care.

- Communicate proactively - Update clients about arrival times, route issues, or delays.

- Go the extra mile - Little gestures like helping load/unload show you aim to be a partner.

By consistently demonstrating your professionalism and value, you'll earn repeat customers and referrals. A stellar reputation in the trucking community can fuel incredible growth.

With dedication and smart planning, you have all the ingredients for trucking success. Of course, the open road ahead will throw some curves and potholes your way. But by leveraging these beginner tips, you'll smoothly shift gears and hit the highway of your dreams. Now let's get truckin'!

CHAPTER 1: UNDERSTANDING THE TRUCKING INDUSTRY

The Role of Trucking in the Global Economy

Imagine for a moment a world without trucks. Store shelves sit empty. Manufacturing plants idle. Construction projects halt. The global supply chain - the lifeblood of trade and commerce - grinds to a standstill. But luckily we live in a world powered by trucking. This vital industry keeps our economy rolling.

As a beginner looking to enter the trucking profession, it's important to understand the indispensable role trucks play in domestic and international trade. Whether transporting raw materials or finished products, the trucking industry enables the efficient movement of goods worldwide.

Linking Manufacturers to Marketplaces

Trucks provide the critical transportation link between manufacturers and retailers. Imagine appliances rolling off the assembly line. Without trucks, those refrigerators have no route to the appliance store. Trucks collect goods from factories and warehouses and efficiently deliver them to where they need to go.

Connecting Rural Communities

Farmers in rural areas rely on trucks to transport their crops, dairy, and livestock to processing plants and urban population centers. Trucks enable food grown in remote locations to nourish people and livestock worldwide.

Building the World

The construction industry depends on trucks to receive everything from concrete and lumber to heavy equipment and scaffolding. Trucks keep build sites stocked with materials and drive economic growth by facilitating development.

Responding to Disasters

When disasters strike, trucks deliver critical supplies and aid. From bottled water and blankets to generators and debris removal, trucks provide logistical support in times of crisis. They're often the first responders to get communities on the road to recovery.

Fueling International Trade

On an international scale, enormous container ships may steer globalization, but trucks power the system from docks to distribution centers. Trucks transport imported goods across borders and continents. Without them, ships would have nowhere to unload their valuable cargo.

Empowering Small Businesses

Trucking services help smaller companies transport products when they don't have their own fleet. This provides access to wider distribution and new markets. Trucking thereby promotes healthy competition and economic diversity.

As you can see, trucking forms the supply chain backbone that supports commerce and trade worldwide. By choosing a career in trucking, you're boarding for an adventure that keeps the global economy thriving. You'll join the worldwide community of truck drivers who collectively deliver prosperity and growth both at home and abroad. So when opportunity knocks offering a trucking job, grab the wheel knowing you'll drive progress across borders.

Trends and Growth Potential in Trucking

With the rise of e-commerce and increasing global trade, the trucking industry is poised for tremendous growth. As a beginner looking to launch your trucking career, it's important to understand the key trends shaping the future of this dynamic field. By arming yourself with insight into emerging technologies and evolving business needs, you'll drive your career in an advantageous direction.

Let's explore some of the top trends and growth potentials transforming trucking:

Leveraging Logistics Technology

Innovations in logistics technology are creating new opportunities to optimize efficiency. Solutions like route optimization software, load matching services, and supply chain tracking systems allow carriers to transport more freight in less time. Adopting these tools can boost productivity and profits.

Autonomous Trucking

Self-driving trucks may one day become mainstream, but for now the technology is still emerging. Many experts believe autonomous vehicles will complement rather than replace human drivers in the near-term. This could allow you to focus on higher-level logistics while your truck handles basic highway driving.

Sustainability

Eco-conscious consumers and green government initiatives are increasing demand for sustainable trucking options. Carriers who invest in fuel efficiency, transition to alternative fuels, or adopt zero-emissions transportation will have a market advantage.

Specialized Services

The proliferation of e-commerce is fueling specialized delivery services for oversized items, time-sensitive freight, and final mile residential delivery. Specializing in a niche service area can help smaller carriers compete with large fleets.

Shifting Demographics

As online shopping explodes, trucking demand is projected to grow across all consumer sectors. And a shortage of younger drivers provides an opportunity for a new generation to power the industry forward.

Expanded Training

In response to the driver shortage, many carriers now offer paid CDL training programs. Take advantage of a company-sponsored program to cover the cost of licensing and quickly get your wheels rolling.

Strong Freight Demand

Due to rising e-commerce, manufacturing activity, and construction projects, freight volume is predicted to increase significantly over the next decade. More trucks will be needed to meet shipping demand.

By getting a head start on understanding key trends in trucking, you'll shift your budding career into overdrive. Look for opportunities to implement cutting-edge tools, master specialized services, and demonstrate enthusiasm for the industry. The road ahead looks bright for the next generation of drivers. So buckle up and let's truck into the future!

Key Players and Competitive Landscape

As a beginner in trucking, understanding the competitive landscape will help you navigate your career wisely. The trucking industry is comprised of carriers large and small, but is dominated by several major corporations. Getting to know these industry titans and how they differentiate themselves will provide useful context.

Let's look at some of the key players:

J.B. Hunt

Founded in 1961 in Arkansas, J.B. Hunt has grown into one of the largest transportation companies in North America. They operate over 12,000 trucks and 78,000 trailers across the contiguous U.S. J.B. Hunt specializes in providing dependable truckload and intermodal freight solutions.

Knight-Swift

Headquartered in Arizona, Knight-Swift operates the largest tractor fleet in North America with over 23,000 trucks. Their services include refrigerated, dry van, and flatbed freight delivery. Through mergers and acquisitions, they've rapidly expanded their reach and capacity.

Schneider National

This Wisconsin-based carrier dates back to 1935. Schneider operates nearly 11,000 trucks and 48,000 trailers. They are an industry leader in driver training programs, electric fleet vehicles, and logistics technology.

Estes Express Lines

Founded in 1931 in Virginia, Estes offers a wide range of shipping services within the eastern U.S. They operate over 7,500 trucks and more than 27,000 trailers out of over 200 terminals. Estes specializes in time-critical shipping for industrial and commercial clients.

XPO Logistics

XPO provides freight transportation across multiple modes: truckload, less than truckload, intermodal, drayage, last mile, and more. Based in Connecticut with operations across Europe and Asia, XPO Logistics owns over 16,000 tractors and 46,000 trailers globally.

In addition to these large carriers, small fleets and independent owner-operators make up a significant share of the trucking industry. They offer specialized services within niche regions and clients. By leveraging flexibility and forging close customer relationships, smaller trucking companies thrive alongside giants like J.B. Hunt and Schneider.

As you jumpstart your career, observing how top carriers structure their operations and services can help you identify potential opportunities. But don't discount the strong role small fleets continue to play. With grit and determination, an independent trucker can still compete and succeed in this diverse industry. Buckle up and shift gears as we truck into the future!

CHAPTER 2: CRAFTING YOUR BUSINESS PLAN

Defining Your Trucking Business Concept

You have your CDL, DOT authority, and are eager to launch your own trucking company. But before purchasing that first rig, you need a solid business concept. Defining your niche, services, and target market will determine if your company thrives or stalls on the side of the road.

Let's explore key steps for defining your unique trucking business:

Identify Your Niche

Will you focus on local deliveries or long-haul routes? What type of freight will you specialize in transporting? Pinpointing your niche helps attract ideal customers. Consider these common trucking niches:

- Construction - Hauling heavy equipment and materials to job sites.

- Agriculture - Transporting crops, livestock, and farm supplies.

- Fuel - Delivering gasoline, diesel, and other fluids. Requires a hazmat endorsement.

- Auto - Shipping newly manufactured vehicles long distances.

- Refrigerated - Hauling perishable frozen and fresh foods across the country.

- General Freight - A flexible option for hauling a wide range of dry goods.

Your niche can evolve over time. But starting targeted helps establish your reputation and expertise.

Determine Services Offered

Outline the exact trucking services you will provide. This could include:

- Long-haul, cross-country shipping

- Short-haul, local delivery

- Full Truckload (FTL) - Entire trailer used by one shipper

- Less than Truckload (LTL) - Trailer with freight from multiple shippers

- Flatbed, reefer, dry van, or tanker trailer transport

- Loading/unloading assistance

- 24/7 emergency roadside service

- Storage and warehousing

List all services that distinguish your company and meet customer needs.

Identify Target Customers

Which shippers will contract your company's services? Be specific. For example:

- Small construction firms contracting projects within a 150 mile radius.

- Regional poultry processors shipping to major supermarket chains.

- Local dairy farmers cooperative transporting to commercial cheese plants.

- Mom-and-pop furniture makers shipping hand-crafted goods nationwide.

Understanding your ideal customer profile allows tailored marketing.

Calculate Costs

Determine pricing for your services that covers expenses and generates profit:

- Factor in costs: insurance, maintenance, fuel, truck payments, driver salaries, etc.

- Research current industry rates in your region. Don't severely undercut.

- Price competitively to attract customers while sustaining your business.

- Offer discounts for frequent shippers or those with high volume.

Having a clear picture of your costs and pricing model keeps your company financially viable.

By defining your niche, services, target market, and costs you pave the way for trucking success. Your business concept is the roadmap that guides all future decisions. Follow it faithfully as you shift your dreams into drive.

Market Analysis and Strategy

You've defined your trucking niche and services. But launching a successful company requires in-depth market analysis and a strategic marketing plan. By understanding your competitive landscape and crafting targeted promotional campaigns, you can gain traction and accelerate your growth.

Conduct a Market Analysis

Before marketing your services, analyze your regional trucking industry:

- Identify direct competitors and study their operations, pricing, and services. This reveals where you can differentiate.

- Talk to shippers to learn their pain points and assess unmet transportation needs you can fulfill.

- Research industry reports detailing freight trends, regulations, and economic conditions shaping your market.

- Seek qualified brokers to connect you with shippers. They become invaluable marketing partners.

- Look for promising new customer segments, such as manufacturers expanding locally.

An insightful market analysis illuminates opportunities to profitably deliver value.

Craft Your Marketing Plan

Now develop a comprehensive marketing strategy to attract your ideal customers:

- Define your brand identity and messaging. What makes your company unique?

- Leverage your website and social media to demonstrate expertise. Share content that engages followers.

- Run targeted digital ads promoting your services to local shippers.

- Design eye-catching truck graphics to spark interest when out on the roads.

- Print brochures, flyers and business cards to distribute within your network.

- Cold call, email, and visit potential customers to introduce your services.

- Attend local trade shows and networking events to connect with shippers face-to-face.

- Partner with complementary companies to cross-promote each other.

A multifaceted marketing campaign gets your brand noticed and remembered.

Gauge Effectiveness

Continuously measure your marketing results and refine tactics accordingly. Track metrics like website traffic, ad clicks, and customer leads generated. Pivot strategies that aren't working. Capitalize on those yielding outcomes.

Conducting diligent market research, developing a strategic marketing plan, and gauging performance ensures your efforts and investments deliver maximum impact. Follow these steps to gain momentum and shift your trucking business into overdrive.

Financial Projections and Funding Requirements

You have a solid trucking business plan—but do you have the funds to put it in motion? Carefully projecting costs and revenue, determining financing needs, and securing capital are essential steps for launching your venture. This chapter will guide you through the key financial considerations for getting your wheels rolling.

Building Your Financial Model

Develop a comprehensive pro forma projecting realistic costs and income:

- Estimate fixed and variable operating expenses. Factor in fuel, maintenance, insurance, salaries, loan payments, etc.

- Research typical profit margins in your niche. Use this to forecast realistic revenue.

- Make conservative assumptions, especially when starting out. It's easier to adjust upward later.

- Project cash flow, profit and loss, and balance sheet statements for the first 12-24 months.

- Run worst-case scenario models in case volumes or margins underperform.

Your financial projections identify how much funding you'll require.

Exploring Funding Options

With funding needs defined, determine the best financing sources for your situation:

- Self-finance through personal savings, home equity, or assets if possible. This avoids debt obligations.

- Seek loans from banks or the Small Business Administration. Weigh repayment terms carefully.

- Consider business partners who can invest capital and share risk.

- Research trucking-specific financing programs through truck dealers and manufacturers.

- Crowdfund startup costs by making your pitch to the crowd.

- Apply for small business grants if you qualify. These provide free funding.

A prudent mix of funding sources will provide sufficient working capital until your company gains traction.

Pitching Investors

If seeking loans or equity partners, you'll need to craft a compelling funding request:

- Quantify the strong demand for your niche in the target market.

- Emphasize your competitive edge through specialized services, prices, or capabilities.

- Outline growth milestones and KPIs to illustrate your expansion strategy.

- Highlight your industry expertise and preparedness to execute the operating plan.

- Be transparent about risks and have contingency plans to reassure investors.

With a solid pitch deck and financial model, you can fuel your trucking dreams. Careful financial planning converts your vision into an engine that drives profits.

Chapter 3: Legal Framework and Compliance

Choosing the Right Business Structure

You have a vision for an amazing trucking company—but how will you actually set up and register your business? Choosing the right structure is a key legal decision that impacts everything from taxes to liability exposure. This chapter will explore structures for trucking ventures to help guide your choice.

Sole Proprietorship

The simplest option is operating as a sole proprietorship. This means the business has no separate legal identity—it is owned and operated by you personally.

Pros:

☐ Easy and inexpensive to register. Just file "doing business as" paperwork.

- You retain complete control over operations.

- Business income and losses flow through to your personal tax return.

Cons:

- You have unlimited personal liability for all debts and claims against the business. Risky!

- Restricted ability to raise investment capital compared to other structures.

- Limits business continuity in case of your death or incapacity.

Limited Liability Company (LLC)

LLCs are a very popular choice for small trucking companies.

Pros:

- Liability protection separates your personal assets from the business.

- More credibility with customers than sole proprietorships.

- Ownership flexibility through managing members vs passive investors.

Cons:

- More complex to establish with state filing requirements.

- Requires drafting an operating agreement.

- Self-employment taxes still apply.

Corporation

Establishing your trucking venture as a C-corp or S-corp is better suited for larger, growth-focused companies.

Pros:

- Limit liability for shareholders.

- Facilitates attracting outside investors.

- Separate corporate tax rules can yield benefits.

Cons:

- Most expensive and paperwork-intensive to set up and maintain.

- Require corporate formalities like shareholder meetings, directors, etc.

- Double taxation of profits for C-corps.

Carefully weigh the pros and cons of each structure against your business goals. An LLC offers a good middle ground of liability protection without major complexity for most trucking startups. Consult an accountant and attorney to ensure you choose the optimal framework. The right foundation allows your trucking dreams to safely take to the open roads.

Necessary Licenses, Permits, and Registrations

Before hitting the open road, your trucking company must secure key credentials. Navigating permitting and compliance as a beginner can be daunting. This chapter will map out the essential licenses, permits, and registrations needed to legally operate.

Commercial Driver's License (CDL)

An approved CDL is mandatory for all drivers-for-hire. Obtaining this specialized license requires:

- Studying the CDL manual and passing written exams on driving rules and vehicle systems.

- Demonstrating proficiency inspecting trucks and maneuvering a rig through skills tests.

- Completing a medical evaluation by an approved physician.

- Maintaining a clean driving record meeting minimum standards.

DOT Number Registration

You must register for a U.S. Department of Transportation (DOT) number operating commercial vehicles across state lines. This allows roadside inspection and enforcement. Apply easily online.

Motor Carrier Authority

Interstate trucking companies must secure motor carrier operating authority from the Federal Motor Carrier Safety Administration (FMCSA). You'll need:

- MC number - Your unique motor carrier identification number

- USDOT number - Links your company to its vehicles

- BOC-3 - Certifies you have adequate insurance coverage

Intrastate Operating Authority

For in-state trucking, register for operating authority from your state transportation or commerce agency instead of the FMCSA. Each state has unique processes.

IFTA Fuel Tax Credentials

Register for the International Fuel Tax Agreement (IFTA) to legally purchase diesel fuel for interstate use without paying duplicative state taxes. This simplifies compliance.

HVUT Payment

The Heavy Vehicle Use Tax (HVUT) is an annual federal excise tax paid for trucks 55,000 pounds and over. This must be paid to the IRS.

Oversize/Overweight Permits

If hauling oversized or heavy loads, obtain special permits from all states where the load will pass through. Requirements vary.

Thoroughly research and complete every necessary approval, license, and permit. Skirting compliance carries steep fines and risks operations. But clearing all regulatory hurdles paves the way to legally and safely steer your trucking company down the open road.

Understanding and Complying with Regulations

As a new trucking entrepreneur, operating legally requires familiarizing yourself with key regulations and compliance obligations. While complex, these rules exist primarily to promote safety, accountability, and fair competition. Making compliance second nature protects your company.

Key Federal Regulations

FMCSRs - The Federal Motor Carrier Safety Regulations oversee virtually all interstate trucking requirements for safe vehicles, driving standards, load securement, hazmat transportation, and more. Know them inside and out!

Hours of Service (HOS) - Strict logbook requirements regulate when and how long drivers can be on duty to prevent fatigue-related accidents. Time is tracked in 14-hour windows.

CSA - The Compliance, Safety, Accountability program monitors carrier performance using roadside inspections and crash data. Unsafe outcomes can lead to interventions or audits.

FMUTCD - The Federal Motor Vehicle Transportation Construction Driving manual sets national standards for work zone safety and temporary traffic control policies.

ADA - The Americans with Disabilities Act mandates accessibility for disabled truck drivers. Accommodations must be provided when reasonable.

State and Local Laws

In addition to federal regulations, adhere to all state, county, and city commercial driving laws in your operating region, such as:

- Truck weight, height, and length limits

- Chain laws during winter weather

- Load securement and covering rules

- Emission standards and anti-idling ordinances

- Traffic patterns, parking restrictions, and speed limits

Staying Current

Regulations frequently evolve, so staying up-to-date on requirements is crucial through:

- Reading the Federal Register announcements

- Participating in local trucking associations

- Attending DOT seminars and workshops

- Subscribing to news updates from commercial carrier services

Mastering the regulatory environment protects your company and shows you operate at the highest standards. Never hesitate to seek clarification from officials if an obligation is unclear. Compliance in trucking requires lifelong learning. But keeping it your top priority smooths the journey for all.

CHAPTER 4: FINANCING YOUR TRUCKING BUSINESS

Options for Raising Capital

You have a dynamite business plan ready to launch. But turning your trucking dreams into reality requires capital. This chapter will explore funding options accessible to beginners so you can get rolling.

Bootstrapping

Bootstrapping means relying on personal funds to initially finance your venture. Advantages include:

- Avoiding interest payments and giving up equity prematurely

- Forcing discipline by having a limited budget

- Demonstrating commitment by putting your own money at stake

Of course, bootstrapping limits your runway. But it remains a common startup approach.

Crowdfunding

Crowdfunding platforms like Kickstarter and Indiegogo allow making an online pitch to potential backers globally. You set a fundraising minimum and timeline. If successful, contributors provide startup cash in exchange for future products or equity.

Government Programs

The Small Business Administration offers beneficial financing programs including:

- SBA 7(a) Loans geared to trucking companies

- SBA Express Loans up to $25,000

- Microloans up to $50,000

- Women-owned, veteran-owned, and minority-owned business grants

Explore every relevant public funding option before considering expensive private financing.

Business Loans

Traditional bank loans provide flexible capital but require strong personal credit, collateral, and proven experience. Expect thorough vetting and restrictions on use of funds.

Alternative lenders like Kabbage and BlueVine offer quicker, easier business loans and lines of credit. But their rates are steep.

Invoice Factoring

Invoice factoring lets you borrow against unpaid customer invoices to generate working capital. Companies like BlueVine provide trucking factoring services at competitive rates. It smoothes cash flow but doesn't help long-term growth.

Angel Investors

Wealthy individuals provide startup capital in exchange for convertible debt or equity. Make connections through local investor networks and pitch events. Ideal for expanding established trucking companies.

Carefully weighing the pros and cons of funding approaches allows wise access to growth capital as a beginner. Your choices pave the road to success.

Cost Management and Budgeting

Launching a profitable trucking company requires meticulous tracking and management of costs. Creating a realistic budget and monitoring performance prepares you to navigate the financial road ahead. Let's explore essential tips for minimizing expenses and maximizing margins.

Building Your Budget

A detailed budget estimates costs and revenue month-by-month during your first year:

- Forecast expenses like equipment purchases, licensing, maintenance, fuel, insurance, and debt payments.

- Estimate income conservatively until your revenue model is proven.

- Include a 10-20% buffer for unforeseen expenses.

- Use past financial statements from similar companies as a model.

- Continuously update the budget as you refine projections.

Your budget steers you away from financial trouble.

Trim Variable Costs

Actively monitor and reduce variable costs that fluctuate with business volume like:

- Fuel - Invest in efficient trucks. Set optimal routes and speeds. Perform maintenance to boost mpg. Use apps to find the cheapest diesel.

- Labor - Take advantage of independent contractors instead of employees until volume is consistent.

- Maintenance & Repairs - Institute meticulous preventative maintenance schedules and promptly address issues.

- Tolls & Fees - Review routes to minimize tolls. Pay registration fees on time to avoid penalties.

Small savings add up!

Control Fixed Costs

Fixed costs remain constant regardless of volume. Manage carefully by:

- Negotiating office and yard leases with slow escalations and flexible terms

- Securing insurance through carriers offering newcomer discounts

- Buying quality used trucks to avoid large depreciation hits

- Financing equipment at competitive rates and payment structures

Monthly monitoring against your budget identifies problems early so you can take corrective actions if needed. Consistent cost control keeps you on the road to profitability.

Insurance and Risk Management

Operating commercial trucks involves substantial liability. As a beginner, it's crucial to implement prudent risk management through comprehensive insurance coverage, safety protocols, and more. This chapter outlines key policies and practices for shielding your assets.

Essential Coverages

Secure adequate commercial auto liability insurance protecting from:

- Bodily injury and property damage claims

- Accidents involving uninsured motorists

- Physical damage coverage for owned trucks and equipment

Also obtain:

- General liability insurance covering your facilities, clients, and employees

- Cargo insurance to pay for damaged or stolen freight

- Workers' compensation for employees

Match coverage limits and deductibles to your size and risk tolerance. Work with a broker specializing in the trucking industry.

Safety First

Reduce claims by making safety your top priority:

- Only employ experienced, licensed drivers with clean records

- Implement extensive new driver training programs

- Equip trucks with collision avoidance technologies

- Establish truck speed limits and no-cell-phone policies

- Require prompt accident and violation reporting

Your premiums will benefit from a strong safety culture.

Tighten Contracts

Include adequate indemnity and insurance requirements in all customer and vendor contracts to transfer liability exposure. Require COIs.

Manage Cash Flow

Get invoices out promptly and accelerate collections to minimize open receivables. This reduces credit risk and ensures liquidity to pay claims quickly.

Conduct Audits

Perform periodic audits checking for compliance with regulations and internal safety policies. Identify any deficiencies immediately for correction. Documentation protects you.

By combining prudent insurance with proactive risk management tactics, you can confidently drive into the future knowing protection is in place. Don't cut corners on safeguarding your assets.

CHAPTER 5: ACQUIRING YOUR FLEET

New vs. Used Trucks: Evaluating Your Options

One of the biggest startup decisions in trucking is acquiring your inaugural rig. Do you splurge on a shiny new truck or opt for an experienced used vehicle? This chapter will guide you through valuating new versus used trucks to select the ideal option.

Reasons to Go New

New trucks offer compelling advantages:

- Latest engine and amenities for maximum productivity

- Under full warranty for repairs and maintenance

- No inheritied issues or unknown history of abuse

- Custom configuration to your precise specifications

- Financing incentives often offered for first-time owners

- Enhanced driver satisfaction and company image

But new trucks come at a steep price.

Reasons to Buy Used

Alternatively, purchasing used provides benefits like:

- Significantly lower upfront investment

- Opportunity to pay cash rather than financing

- Ability to afford additional trucks faster

- Minimal depreciation since the largest losses already occurred

- Inspection can reveal existing wear and maintenance needs

However, used trucks present greater risks of mechanical problems and shorter remaining useful life.

Key Considerations

Weigh options by:

- Comparing total lifetime costs, not just initial price

- Testing used trucks extensively prior to purchase

- Having a mechanic inspect the engine, transmission, etc.

- Reviewing full maintenance records when available

- Forecasting lost revenue from potential downtime

- Considering customer perception and driver experience

Run the numbers on both scenarios. Often a 2-3 year old truck with 50,000 miles offers the ideal balance of quality and affordability.

Whether new or used, choose your trucks wisely. This decision impacts productivity and profitability for years down the road.

Leasing vs. Buying: What's Best for Your Business

Purchasing your trucking fleet outright provides control and equity. But leasing offers flexibility and lower risk. How do you choose? This chapter weighs the pros and cons of each approach to guide your decision making.

Reasons to Purchase Your Trucks

Buying your own trucks has advantages including:

- You retain ownership and can sell the assets later

- Avoids lease restrictions on usage and maintenance

- Builds business equity as trucks appreciate

- Loans may have lower payments than leases

- Tax benefits like depreciation deductions

However, purchases tie up substantial capital.

Reasons to Lease Your Trucks

Alternatively, leasing trucks can be smart because:

- Conserves startup capital for other expenses

- May offer lower monthly payments than financing

- Maintenance may be bundled into lease terms

- Shorter lease periods provide flexibility

- Lets you easily scale fleet size to demand

- Lessor bears risk of disposal and residual value

But leasing forfeits equity and ownership.

Key Factors to Consider

Carefully evaluate your situation by:

- Comparing total cost of leasing vs buying over likely duration

- Considering how long you plan to keep trucks in service

- Assessing maintenance preferences and capabilities

- Reviewing lease terms like mileage limits and condition requirements

- Determining your tax and accounting preferences

- Analyzing cash flow to fund down payments if buying

For many startups, leasing provides an attractive low-risk introduction to fleet ownership. But running the numbers for your specific needs takes the guesswork out.

Whether buying or leasing, structure agreements thoughtfully to control costs and ensure the flexibility your business requires. With wise planning, you'll be off and trucking efficiently.

Maintenance and Upkeep of Your Vehicles

A profitable trucking company depends on keeping rigs rolling safely down the highway. Don't learn the hard way that neglecting maintenance results in headaches and lost revenue. This chapter outlines tips to make vehicle care second nature.

Schedule Regular Servicing

Routinely perform:

- Oil changes based on mileage intervals, not just time. Use manufacturer specs.

- Tire rotations during oil changes to maximize tread life.

- Annual fluid flushes and filter replacements.

- Routine inspections checking belts, hoses, steering components, etc.

- Windshield wiper replacements every 6 months.

Scheduling maintenance proactively reduces roadside breakdowns.

Inspect Daily

Drivers should conduct thorough pre- and post-trip inspections covering:

- Fluid levels - Lights

- Brake operation - Tire condition

- Suspension parts - Safety reflectors

- Leaks/hoses - Load securement

Identify issues immediately to schedule shop repairs.

Perform Enroute Checks

During extended hauls, routinely check:

- Instrument gauges for temperature/pressure alerts

- Undercarriage for dragging parts or looseness

- Wheels for abnormal heat indicating brake problems

- Cargo for shifting/damage

This prevents problems from escalating undetected.

Address Issues ASAP

Never delay diagnosis and repair of mechanical problems. A failure on the road can be catastrophic. Prioritize:

- Check engine lights - Strange noises

- Oil leaks - Vibrations

- Brake problems - Lack of power

A trusted mechanic and spare parts source is invaluable.

Practice preventative maintenance religiously. Letting upkeep slide leads to harmful breakdowns, safety issues, and expensive repairs down the road. Your vehicles are your business lifeblood—treat them accordingly.

CHAPTER 6: OPERATIONS AND LOGISTICS

Setting Up Your Operations Base

As an owner-operator, your truck serves as your mobile office. But launching a company with multiple trucks requires establishing a home operations base. This chapter covers how to set up a functional, cost-efficient terminal or yard.

Location Considerations

Seeking a base, prioritize:

- Proximity to customers for efficient access

- Reasonable commute for drivers

- Expandability to accommodate growth

- Access to main highways and routes

- Favorable zoning allowing trucking activity

- Costs within budget

Lease or Buy?

Leasing provides flexibility, but buying a yard builds equity. Weigh trade-offs like:

- Available capital or financing

- Current commercial real estate rates and terms in your area

- Long-term plans for company size and location

Start small by leasing, then buy once established.

Facility Requirements

Basic must-haves for a terminal:

- Office space for staff and records

- Driver lounge and locker room

- Parking for trucks and employee vehicles

- Fenced secure yard for equipment

- Sufficient power supply and lighting

- Restrooms and basic kitchen amenities

Customize to suit your niche - like hazmat storage or refrigeration.

Operational Considerations

Also set up:

- Communication systems like phones, radios, WiFi

- Routing and tracking software

- Safety equipment like cameras, alarms, fire suppression

- Navigation and telematics systems in trucks

- A shop or access to vehicle maintenance

- Load securing and lifting equipment

Creating an efficient, comfortable home base cultivates team productivity and morale. Take the time to set up your operations hub thoughtfully.

Routing and Scheduling for Efficiency

Profitability in trucking depends on maximizing loads and minimizing empty miles. Careful route optimization and trip scheduling prevents wasted time and fuel. This chapter shares tips for beginners to boost efficiency.

Optimize Your Routing

- Use GPS and route planning apps to map fastest legal routes accounting for road conditions, trafflc, construction, etc.

- Plan for mandatory 30-minute breaks every 8 hours to stay compliant with hours of service regulations.

- Identify optimal fuel stops, weigh stations, and rest areas along the route.

- Sequence multi-stop trips to avoid retracing steps.

- Review routes regularly for new shortcuts, roundabouts, or exits.

- Share route details with drivers to keep trips consistent.

Efficient routing promotes safety while cutting costs.

Schedule Wisely

- Use a load board to identify backhaul opportunities near planned destinations.

- Accept loads giving you experience in new, profitable regions to expand your network.

- Avoid scheduling deliveries during high-traffic times that will extend trip length.

- Build buffer time into commitments to account for potential delays.

- Cluster orders going to the same destination when possible.

- Sequence orders logically based on location, priority, and pickup/delivery windows.

Thoughtful trip scheduling keeps customers satisfied and revenue flowing.

Leverage Technology

Tools like transportation management systems, GPS, and ELDs provide data to refine routes and schedules continuously. Analyze past trips to spot redundancies. Driver feedback also identifies inefficiencies.

Every mile saved goes straight to your bottom line. Make routing optimization and smart scheduling core competencies right from the start.

Implementing Technology in Your Operations

Launching a trucking company today means tapping the power of modern technology across your operations. Implementing the right solutions will boost efficiency, compliance, and competitiveness. This chapter shares tips for a beginner.

Tools for Drivers

Equip your trucks and drivers with:

- Electronic logging devices (ELDs) to log hours of service and duty status digitally - it's legally mandated.

- Two-way communication systems like radios or push-to-talk apps.

- Navigation/GPS tracking to monitor location and route progress.

- Fleet management apps to receive orders, route details, compliance alerts, etc.

- Cab cameras to record incidents and exonerate drivers.

Technology improves safety and accountability on the road.

Back Office Systems

Optimize headquarters and management functions with:

- Load boards to find loads and manage brokerage.

- Accounting and invoicing software to control finances.

- Real-time shipment tracking and notifications for customers.

- Equipment monitoring for engine diagnostics and preventative maintenance.

- Data analytics to gain business insights.

Automating admin tasks allows focusing resources on customers and growth.

Future Proof Yourself

Also stay on the cutting edge by:

- Researching emerging transportation technologies at tradeshows.

- Testing promising new hardware with a couple trucks first.

□ Getting certified in new mandatory software rollouts proactively.

□ Developing tech troubleshooting capabilities in-house through manuals and training.

Integrating technology early will serve your company well. But ensure solutions genuinely address specific pain points in your operations. The learning curve is steep, but mastery pays dividends.

CHAPTER 7: BUILDING YOUR BRAND AND MARKETING

Developing a Strong Brand Identity

Beyond operating trucks, succeeding in trucking means building a memorable brand. Developing a professional identity engenders trust and distinction. This chapter shares branding tips for beginners seeking to stand out.

Start with Your Story

Define your origin story and values. Share what makes your company special:

- Are you fulfilling a family trucking legacy?

- Working to empower minority or women drivers?

- Focused on sustainable operations?

- Committed to supporting local businesses?

Your unique narrative forms the branding foundation.

Create a Great Name

Select a name that communicates your specialty or values:

- Include "Trucking", "Freight", "Logistics" or related terms so prospects immediately understand your industry.

- Adds words highlighting your niche like "Livestock", "Expedited" or "Hazmat".

- Evokes ideas of trustworthiness, safety, or experience based on your goals.

- Is memorable and easy to spell to aid marketing and referrals.

If available, secure matching .com and social media usernames.

Design a Logo

Your logo visually represents your brand. Keep it simple, recognizable, and meaningful by:

- Using your company name or initials as the focal point. Add est. [year] for authority.

- Incorporating symbols of your niche like road images, trucks, livestock, crops, etc.

- Choosing 2-4 complementary colors reflecting your identity.

- Including key brand taglines if they strengthen recognition.

Apply the logo consistently across all marketing materials, communications, signage and of course, your trucks.

Define Your Personality

What voice and style best fits your brand? Craft communications expressing your uniqueness:

- Friendly and folksy or serious and professional?

- Focused on customer service, innovation, or community?

- Written in conversational or corporate tone?

- Utilizing industry lingo and jargon or plain, simple language?

Let your brand personality genuinely reflect corporate culture for authenticity. This forms lasting brand affinity enabling growth.

Effective Marketing Strategies for Trucking

With your trucks, license, insurance and systems in place, securing a steady stream of loads requires strategic marketing. Combining digital outreach with relationship selling will get your business noticed. This chapter shares tactical tips to turbocharge your trucking marketing.

Build a Compelling Website

Your website establishes credibility 24/7. Make it user-friendly and impactful with:

- An "About Us" page sharing your founding story and values.

- Detailed pages flaunting your services, equipment, drivers and safety record.

- Strong calls-to-action to request quotes or contact sales.

- Blog/news section with helpful industry content.

- Prominent contact info and online load request forms.

Don't cut corners on design - this represents your brand.

Harness the Power of Search

Employ search engine optimization to get found locally:

- Target relevant keywords around your location and specialty - like "Dallas refrigerated trucking".

- Update site content frequently including those terms.

- Claim and optimize Google Business and other directory listings.

- Build local links and citations to strengthen SEO authority.

This helps you rank higher in searches.

Go Social

Promote business milestones and achievements through:

- A professional Facebook business page.

- Sharing content on LinkedIn to establish expertise.

- Engaging with potential customers on Twitter.

- Posting photos/videos highlighting your niche on Instagram.

Social platforms expand your digital reach and network cost-efficiently.

Build Word-of-Mouth

Satisfied customers and contacts become ambassadors through referrals. Always:

- Provide 5-star service on every haul to create advocates.

- Request introductions to other prospects they work with.

- Ask for online reviews, testimonials, and referrals you can market with.

Nothing drives new business like recommendations from trusted peers.

Consistent marketing paired with delivering for customers will perpetually fill your trailer. Stay dedicated in good times and bad - momentum compounds over time!

Digital Marketing and Social Media Presence

In addition to over-the-road experience, today's trucking entrepreneurs need digital marketing savvy. Building your online presence establishes credibility and expanded reach. This chapter shares tips for novices to drive growth through digital channels.

Optimized Website

Ensure your website offers a strong first impression by:

- Using high-quality photos of your equipment, team, and loads.

- Including detailed pages highlighting your services, safety record, and expertise.

- Featuring testimonials from satisfied customers.

- Publishing helpful "how-to" articles showcasing knowledge.

- Ensuring fast load times, easy navigation, and mobile responsiveness.

This makes conversion easier when prospects visit.

Search Engine Visibility

Improving local SEO helps potential customers find your site when searching relevant keywords. Tactics include:

- Updating content frequently with target terms.

- Building backlinks from directories, associations, and aggregators.

- Publishing blog posts on industry topics to demonstrate thought leadership.

- Monitoring search rankings routinely to address drops.

Combining great content with solid SEO generates steady traffic.

Social Media Presence

Promote brand awareness on key platforms:

- Share photos, news, and achievements on Facebook.

- Post updates showcasing equipment and expertise on Instagram.

- Join and engage with industry groups on LinkedIn.

- Use Twitter to interact directly with followers and prospects.

Delivering value earns audience engagement and trust over time.

Paid Ads

Supplement organic reach with targeted pay-per-click and social ads focused on your specialties and metro area. Measure conversions to optimize spend.

With a thoughtful online marketing strategy, your business gains visibility and credibility. This amplifies word-of-mouth as satisfied customers spread the word.

CHAPTER 8: SECURING CLIENTS AND CONTRACTS

Networking and Building Industry Relationships

Solving the complex logistics challenges of customers requires collaboration. While new to the industry, actively networking builds relationships that fuel referrals and opportunities. This chapter shares proven networking strategies to integrate yourself in the trucking community.

Attend Industry Events

Join relevant regional and national associations and attend their networking events, tradeshows, and conferences. These provide exposure to:

- Prospective shippers looking for new transportation partners.

- Experienced peers who can provide mentorship and advice.

- Industry innovations you can implement.

- Potential brokers who need reliable carriers.

Come prepared with professional materials to leave memorable first impressions.

Seek Speaking Engagements

Once established, raise your profile by requesting to speak at local trucking industry events on your specialized expertise. Gaining exposure as a thought leader draws business to you.

Volunteer Strategically

Look for volunteer committees and leadership roles in key industry groups:

- This showcases your commitment to the community.

- Working alongside other volunteers fosters relationships with peers.

- Leadership positions highlight your knowledge and credibility.

Giving back also expands your network.

Collaborate With Complementary Companies

Build partnerships with providers serving similar customers:

- Align with a warehousing company to provide integrated services.

- Coordinate with a specialized hauler to expand offerings together.

Strategic partnerships increase opportunities.

Prioritize Referrals

Satisfied customers are invaluable advocates. Systematically request introductions or testimonials from them to gain warm referrals.

Joining the industry conversation through smart networking builds the connections and reputation that enable a startup to thrive. Identify key audiences and engage consistently. Your involvement lays the groundwork for referrals and growth.

Bidding on Contracts and Negotiating Rates

Securing consistent business requires strategic bidding on contracts and negotiating favorable rates with shippers. Avoid leaving money on the table by mastering the art of the deal as a beginner. This chapter shares proven bidding and rate setting strategies.

Know Your Numbers

Calculate your precise operating costs including expenses like:

- Fuel, maintenance, and truck payments

- Driver pay, benefits, training

- Insurance, permits, fees

- Management and administration overhead

This gives you an accurate picture of your fixed and variable costs to build profitable bids.

Set Minimum Profit Margins

Determine the minimum profit margin you need on top of your costs:

- Local hauls may only support 15-20% margins.

- Long distance routes allow margins of 30% or higher.

Sticking to your minimums ensures profitability.

Submit Smart Bids

When bidding for contracts:

- Gather details on load type, frequency, mileage, timing, and destination.

- Factor in costs like return empty miles, loading/unloading time, tolls, etc.

- Weigh competitor bids if disclosed by the shipper.

- Highlight your unique capabilities like hazmat certification.

- Initially bid moderately - you can negotiate downward if needed.

Winning bids balance attractive pricing and communicating your expertise.

Negotiate Win-Win Rates

When brokering one-off loads, look to:

- Make your initial ask at the high end of fair market rate.

- Emphasize your reliability and flawless safety record.

- Offer incentives like top priority handling of their freight.

- Counter just below their best competing offer if needed.

- Accept lower rates on condition they commit to regular volume.

Win-win solutions lead to lasting shipper relationships.

Bidding and negotiations get easier as you gain experience and data. Stay firm on your minimums and you'll secure deals that keep your wheels turning.

Customer Service and Retention Strategies

For small trucking companies, customer retention is imperative to long-term viability. Consistently delivering stellar service earns loyalty even when large fleets undercut you on price. This chapter shares proven customer service practices to set your business apart.

Communicate Proactively

Drivers should provide ongoing status updates during each haul via:

- Notifying dispatch when departing and upon each delivery stop.

- Quickly alerting customers and dispatch about any delays.

- Directly contacting receivers to coordinate arrival times.

This keeps customers informed and head off problems early.

Respond Rapidly

Commit to promptly addressing any customer issues with:

- Fast claim resolution if goods are damaged.

- Quickly remediating service failures like late pickups.

- Answering questions and providing supporting documents for audits or billing disputes.

- Following up to verify issues are fully resolved.

Speedy attention strengthens loyalty.

Ask for Feedback

Routinely survey customers about your performance and solicit suggestions for improvement. Listen carefully and take action on constructive critiques. Follow up to show you took feedback seriously.

Create Relationships

Build rapport with dispatchers and logistics managers by:

- Getting to know them personally and remembering details.

- Participating in community events or associations where you'll connect.

- Sending holiday cards or small gifts of appreciation.

- Celebrating the anniversaries of business relationships annually.

Strong personal connections earn enduring trust.

Go the Extra Mile

Look for opportunities to surprise and delight, like:

- Arriving early or staying late to assist with loading/unloading.

- Providing extra securing supplies as needed for tricky loads.

- Personally thanking them for choosing your company.

Small acts of exceptional service make you unforgettable.

For small carriers, exemplary customer experiences justify your rates and breed referrals. Consistency day-in and day-out cements your status as a valued partner.

Chapter 9: Managing Your Trucking Business

Day-to-Day Operations Management

Once trucks are on the road, the real work begins. Managing schedules, drivers, maintenance and administrative tasks smoothly sets your startup on the path to sustainability. This chapter shares tactics for tackling daily operations.

Centralize Scheduling

Designate an organized dispatcher to handle:

- Monitoring load board postings and arranging backhauls.

- Confirming pickup times with shippers.

- Sequencing multi-stop routes efficiently.

- Providing documentation like BOLs to drivers.

- Resolving any enroute delays or issues promptly.

Dispatcher workflow optimization prevents confusion that slows trucks.

Streamline Maintenance

Create schedules for preventative maintenance tasks like:

- Tire rotations during oil changes.

- Routine fluid flushes and filter changes.

- Annual DOT inspections.

Track maintenance diligently in a log or software. Address issues quickly between hauls to maximize uptime.

Stay Compliant

Update required filings like IFTA quarterly fuel tax reporting. Monitor driver logs and hours of service compliance using ELDs. Conduct safety audits of trucks, equipment, and driving records. Lapses jeopardize your license.

Organize Records

Maintain meticulous files for:

- Driver personnel records like credentials, training, and performance reviews.

- Customer invoices, proof of delivery, dispute information.

- Insurance policies, operating authorities, permits.

Proper documentation protects your business interests.

Motivate Your Team

Keep drivers happy and safe by:

- Recognizing excellent driving records.

- Soliciting input to improve operations.

- Providing bonuses for tenure milestones and referrals.

- Hosting occasional cookouts or events to show appreciation.

Your team's performance fuels the bottom line. Making operations management second nature as a beginner leads to growth and prosperity. Stay organized, attend to details, and keep trucks rolling by taking ownership of daily tasks. Smooth operations form the foundation for expansion.

Human Resources: Hiring and Retention

Skilled drivers and support staff are the lifeblood of a trucking company. As a novice owner, build a stellar team by leveraging best practices in recruiting, hiring, training, and retaining employees. This chapter shares human resources tips tailored to the transportation industry.

Define Key Roles

Determine staffing needs for:

☐ Drivers - CDL Class A for tractor-trailers.

☐ Dispatch coordinators to route trucks.

- Mechanics or partnerships with maintenance shops.

- Operations manager to oversee safety, compliance, etc.

- Administrative staff for billing, accounting, etc.

Write thorough descriptions of required duties, skills, and experience.

Promote Open Positions

Advertise roles through:

- Online job boards targeting the trucking industry.

- Local trade schools with commercial driving programs.

- Sign-on bonuses for driver referrals.

- Your website, social media, and networking contacts.

Cast a wide net to attract qualified applicants.

Interview Strategically

Assess driving records, credentials, work history, communication skills, and temperaments. Gauge comfort working independently and with technology. Validate through reference checks.

Get compliant with regulations by running drug tests, medical exams, and background checks before extending offers.

Onboard Thoroughly

Conduct extensive classroom and on-the-road training for new hires on your operating procedures, safety standards, equipment, and technology. Pair new drivers with experienced mentors initially.

Incentivize Retention

Offer perks like:

- Competitive mileage pay and benefits.

- Bonuses for tenure, referrals, and safe driving records.

- Modern, well-equipped trucks.

- Options for local routes and home time.

Investing in great people provides strong returns through customer satisfaction, safety, and growth.

Scaling Your Business and Growth Strategies

With dedication and hustle as a beginner, you'll be equipped to scale up. Growing sustainably requires planning to add trucks, staff, and customers systematically. This chapter shares smart growth strategies to elevate your trucking company over time.

Add Trucks and Drivers Gradually

Forecast demand growth by:

- Reviewing inquiries and customer feedback on capacity needs.

- Tracking market growth in your geographic area and specialties.

- Monitoring truck utilization rates to identify maximum capacity.

Only lease or purchase additional trucks and hire drivers as justified by revenue expansion. Take things slowly to minimize risk.

Upgrade Facilities

As your fleet expands, invest in:

- Expanded parking, maintenance bays, and amenities at your home terminal.

- Additional owned or leased remote terminals in new strategic markets.

- More advanced transportation management systems and technologies.

Right-sized infrastructure supports efficient scaling.

Broaden Your Customer Base

Pursue new clients through:

- Networking with shippers in booming industries and locations.

- Joining additional load boards and bidding platforms.

- Asking current customers for introductions to their partners.

- Adjusting marketing to attract more small and mid-sized accounts.

Diverse customers prevent reliance on a few large shippers.

Fine-Tune Operations

Review processes to identify and improve pain points. Transition dispatching and maintenance to dedicated teams versus individuals as volume increases. Implement more robust routing software. Streamline HR workflows. Updated systems position you for growth.

Maintain Customer Service

Despite growing, stay visible and hands-on with customers by:

- Directly contacting them about any shipment issues.

- Soliciting regular feedback on your performance as volumes ramp up.

- Assigning standing account reps versus random dispatchers.

Growth without service decline is the ultimate success metric. By scaling strategically, you elevate your company and capabilities over time. The keys are patience, commitment to systems, and focusing on customer satisfaction above all else.

CHAPTER 10: NAVIGATING CHALLENGES AND SETBACKS

Common Roadblocks in the Trucking Business

Turning trucking dreams into reality has challenges. Foreseeing common roadblocks lets you proactively clear the route to success. This chapter outlines frequent pain points novices face and strategies to overcome them.

Securing Funding

New truckers often face financing hurdles obtaining loans or investors. Solutions include:

- Leveraging equipment finance companies that specialize in funding trucks.

- Starting very small and reinvesting revenue until bankable.

- Crowdfunding from community supporters.

- Applying for small business grants and programs.

With perseverance, capital can be accessed.

Recruiting Drivers

The driver shortage makes hiring challenging. Adapt by:

- Training and incentivizing your current drivers to recruit peers.

- Considering viable second chance candidates with past lapses.

- Offering highly competitive pay, benefits, and culture.

- Automating and streamlining processes to ease frustrations.

The right incentives and environment attract talent.

Slow Customer Adoption

When pipelines stall, re-energize outreach through:

- Refreshing marketing targeted to high-potential niches.

- Seeking referrals from your best existing customers.

- Offering discounts or perks for new accounts to incentivize trials.

- Following up persistently to close promising prospects.

Proactive outreach combined with stellar service cultivates customers.

Unpredictable Operating Costs

Volatile fuel, maintenance, and insurance expenses threaten margins. Control costs by:

- Hedging diesel prices through fixed fuel cards.

- Negotiating preferred garage rates through partnerships.

- Instituting strong maintenance programs to prevent repairs.

- Shopping insurance quotes annually to optimize coverage value.

Disciplined financial management preserves profitability.

The path won't always be smooth, but foresight and adaptability keeps your wheels rolling. Leverage available resources and support to power through the common obstacles of starting a trucking company.

Strategies for Overcoming Obstacles

Turning your passion for trucking into a thriving business has challenges. But with grit and adaptability, any roadblock can be overcome. This chapter shares time-tested strategies for tackling common obstacles that stand between beginners and success.

Accessing Startup Financing

Funding trucks, insurance, and systems requires capital. When faced with financing difficulties:

- Start small to prove your model before pursuing loans.

- Seek truck leasing and alternative lenders focused on transportation.

- Crowdfund equipment costs through community connections.

- Apply for every possible grant and small business program.

With perseverance, funding can be secured.

Recruiting Quality Drivers

The driver shortage makes hiring tough. Get creative by:

- Training and incentivizing current drivers to recruit peers.

- Considering second chance drivers where eligible.

- Offering referral bonuses, great culture, and competitive pay.

- Automating to reduce frustrating paperwork.

The right environment and incentives attracts talent.

Gaining Customers

When pipelines stall, reopen doors by:

- Refreshing targeted marketing campaigns.

- Requesting introductions and referrals from current happy clients.

- Following up persistently with promising prospects.

- Offering discounts or perks to incentivize new customer trials.

Proactive outreach paired with great service turns prospects into partners.

Controlling Operating Expenses

Volatile costs threaten margins. Regain control through:

- ☐ Hedging diesel prices via fixed fuel cards.

- ☐ Negotiating preferred garage rates through partnerships.

- ☐ Preventative maintenance to avoid repairs.

- ☐ Regularly re-bidding insurance to optimize value.

With smart financial management, profitability is possible.

Every entrepreneur faces hurdles, but tenacity and adaptability keeps your wheels turning. Leverage available resources and supports to clear any obstacle blocking your path to trucking success.

Milton Keynes UK
Ingram Content Group UK Ltd.
UKHW010708050224
437294UK00018B/757